ISHAQ

LETTERS
FROM A BROKEN GOD

BlueRoseONE.com
Stories Matter
NewDelhi • London

BLUEROSE PUBLISHERS
U.K.

Copyright © Ishaq 2025

All rights reserved by author. No part of this publication may be reproduced, stored in a retrieval system or transmitted in any form or by any means, electronic, mechanical, photocopying, recording or otherwise, without the prior permission of the author. Although every precaution has been taken to verify the accuracy of the information contained herein, the publisher assumes no responsibility for any errors or omissions. No liability is assumed for damages that may result from the use of information contained within.

BlueRose Publishers takes no responsibility for any damages, losses, or liabilities that may arise from the use or misuse of the information, products, or services provided in this publication.

For permissions requests or inquiries regarding this publication, please contact:

BLUEROSE PUBLISHERS
www.BlueRoseONE.com
info@bluerosepublishers.com
+4407342408967

ISBN: 978-93-7018-471-8

Cover design: Daksh
Typesetting: Tanya Raj Upadhyay

First Edition: May 2025

Introduction

Dear Reader,
This is not a book.
It's a graveyard of words I never said.
A thousand unsent messages.
A quiet scream.
A diary written with shaking hands and tear-stained nights.

This is a love story that never got its ending.
A heartbreak that refused to leave silently.
A man who shattered... and kept writing through the dust.

Every Letter in this book was written by someone who loved too much,
lost too deeply,
and healed too slowly.

If you've ever stayed awake wondering if they ever think of you...
if you've ever deleted a message just before pressing send...
if you've ever broken alone in the dark —
these words are for you.

This book is not about getting over them.
It's about finding yourself again
on the other side of the ruin.

—Noah

Connect @wordsbyishaq

Letters from a Broken God

by Ishaq
*A poetic exploration of love, loss, and healing
— one unsent Letter at a time.*

Table of Contents

Letter 1: To the One I Still Write to in Silence 1

Letter 2: The Mug You Left Half Full 3

Letter 3: The Side You Never Slept On........................ 5

Letter 4: The Day You Stopped Talking 7

Letter 5: Your Birthday Without You 9

Letter 6: I Dreamt You Came Back............................. 11

Letter 7: I Still Type Your Name 13

Letter 8: Your Toothbrush Is Still Here 15

Letter 9: I Stopped Playing Our Song...........................17

Letter 10: The Call I Never Made..................................19

Letter 11: You Promised You'd Stay..............................21

Letter 12: I Found Your Hair Tie Today 23

Letter 13: The Day You Walked Out 25

Letter 14: Our Anniversary, Alone.............................. 27

Letter 15: I Tried Loving Someone Else 29

Letter 16: I Wish You Lied...31

Letter 17: I Sat With My Childhood Today................. 33

Letter 18: The 3AM Version of Me 35

Letter 19: You Never Looked Back 37

Letter 20: I Miss Your Voice the Most 39

Letter 21: I Almost Gave Up Today 41

Letter 23: I Deleted Our Photos 45

Letter 24: You Didn't Grieve Me 47

Letter 25: The Night I Almost Texted You 'I Miss You' 49

Letter 26: I Can't Listen to Love Songs Anymore 51

Letter 27: I Stopped Believing in Love 53

Letter 28: I Talked to God About You 55

Letter 29: The Day I Screamed Into a Pillow 57

Letter 30: I Don't Recognize Myself Anymore 59

Letter 31: Maybe It Was My Fault 61

Letter 32: I Should've Held You Tighter That Night 63

Letter 33: I Was Never Enough — Was I? 65

Letter 34: The Last Goodbye You Don't Remember 67

Letter 35: I Still Remember the Way You Looked at Me Once 69

Letter 36: I Heard Your Name Today 71

Letter 37: You Don't Miss Me — I Know That Now .. 73

Letter 38: My Birthday Felt Like a Funeral 75

Letter 39: I Feel Invisible Now 77

Letter 40: I'm Not Sad Anymore — I'm Just Empty 79

Letter 41: I Pretended to Be Okay Today 81

Letter 42: I Let Go of Something Today 83
Letter 43: I Saw You With Someone Else 85
Letter 44: You Replaced Me — I Can't Even Replace My Sleep 87
Letter 45: Dear Me — I'm Sorry 89
Letter 46: I Cleaned the Room Today 91
Letter 47: I Laughed — And Didn't Feel Guilty 93
Letter 48: I Didn't Think About You Until Now 95
Letter 49: I Spoke Kindly to Myself Today 97
Letter 50: I Felt Peace Today — For No Reason 99
Letter 51: To the One I Haven't Met Yet 101
Letter 52: You Taught Me What I Didn't Deserve .. 103
Letter 53: You're Just A Story Now 105
Letter 54: I Don't Need Closure Anymore 107
Letter 55: I Took Myself on a Walk Today 109
Letter 56: I Fell in Love with Silence Again 111
Letter 57: I Think I'm Ready to Love Again Someday 113
Letter 58: Thank You for the Hurt 115
Letter 59: I Forgive You 117
Letter 60: The One I'll Never Send 119
Conclusion 122

Letter 1:
To the One I Still Write to in Silence

I know you'll never read this.
But I write anyway.
Because somewhere between
"I love you"
and
"I lost you"
I forgot how to speak without aching.

That night you left, the rain didn't stop.
You said it made the goodbye feel cleaner.
But I hated that you walked away holding your umbrella,
and I stood there holding your last words.

I'm not writing to win you back.
I'm writing because I'm tired
of choking on unsaid apologies,
and memories that refuse to fade.

You don't need to reply.
I don't even know where to send this.
I just need these words out of me
before they turn into something heavier than silence.

—Noah

Quote

"Some heartbreaks don't scream.
They echo — quietly, endlessly,
in every place that used to feel like home."

Letter 2:
The Mug You Left Half Full

The last time you were here,
you left your tea half-drunk.
Earl Grey. No sugar. Extra milk.
I still remember.

I didn't throw it out.
For three days, I watched it turn cold —
then bitter —
then still.
Like us.

I used to sip from your side of the mug,
thinking maybe I could taste the part of you
that hadn't yet stopped loving me.

Now I sip from silence.

You always said you hated unfinished things.
But you left that cup half-full —
and me
even less.

—Noah

Quote

"It's not the goodbye that breaks us.
It's the things left unfinished —
the tea, the talk, the time."

Letter 3:
The Side You Never Slept On

You never slept on my side of the bed.
But now that you're gone,
even the space you never touched
feels loud.

I fold the blanket over to your side every night —
not out of hope,
but habit.

There's a dent in the mattress
where you never laid your head.
But I still trace it with my palm,
like I'm trying to remember
what missing feels like before it becomes forgetting.

You left behind no goodbye note.
Just that mug by the window —
cold tea, cracked rim,
and the scent of your perfume
soaking into absence.

I never got used to sleeping next to you.
But now,

I can't sleep without imagining
you still do.

—Noah

Quote
*"Absence has a shape.
And it fits perfectly
where love once promised to stay."*

Letter 4:
The Day You Stopped Talking

You didn't block me.
You didn't delete anything.
You just... stopped replying.

That's worse.

I kept checking your "last seen"
like it meant something.
Like maybe your silence was busy,
not brutal.

I said "good morning"
for five days straight.
You didn't say anything.
Even though I know you saw it.

I wanted to call.
But I didn't want to beg.
So I waited.

You never came back.

And that mug you left —
the one with the chipped handle —
I dropped it on purpose last night.

But I still cleaned the pieces.

—Noah

Quote
*"They don't always slam the door.
Sometimes, they just stop knocking."*

Letter 5:
Your Birthday Without You

I bought your favorite cake.
I even played that playlist you loved.

I lit a candle,
not on the cake...
on the table beside your picture.
It felt like a funeral.

I said "happy birthday"
to an empty room.
Then I whispered,
"I still love you."
I didn't mean to.
It just slipped out.

Your perfume is still in the scarf you left behind.
I smell it when I miss your voice.
That's almost every night.

You turned 26 yesterday.

I turned to stone.

—Noah

Quote
"Some birthdays aren't celebrated.
They're survived."

Letter 6:
I Dreamt You Came Back

I saw you last night.
In a dream.

You came home.
You didn't say sorry.
You just held my hand
and made tea
like nothing had happened.

I didn't ask questions.
Because I was scared
you'd vanish if I spoke.

But even in the dream —
I knew you'd leave again.
I could feel it.
Like a clock ticking inside my chest.

Then I woke up.
The room was cold.
The bed was still empty.
The cup was dry.

I sat in that silence
and cried like a boy
who lost something he couldn't name.

Maybe it was love.
Maybe it was you.

Maybe both.

—Noah

Quote

"The worst part isn't waking up alone.
It's remembering they were never coming back."

Letter 7:
I Still Type Your Name

I typed your name into the search bar today.

Just... to see.

Not because I expected anything.
Not because I wanted to talk.
But because forgetting you feels like murder.
And I'm not ready to be a killer.

Your name still auto-fills.
That's what hurts.

I hovered over your old profile picture for too long.
That photo — the one where you're laughing at something I said.
Now I can't remember what it was.

Funny, how I remember your favorite shampoo
but not the last thing that made us laugh.

That's grief, isn't it?
It steals joy first,
then leaves you drowning in details.

—Noah

Quote

*"I don't miss who you are now.
I miss the version of you
that still believed in us."*

Letter 8:
Your Toothbrush Is Still Here

Your toothbrush is still in the holder.

Blue. Soft bristles.
Slightly bent from pressure.

I tried throwing it away once.
I held it over the bin.
But my hand started shaking.

It felt like betrayal.
Like burying someone
while they're still breathing somewhere else.

You once joked that you'd leave a piece of yourself in every place you loved.
You left this toothbrush.
Your bobby pins.
That old hoodie I never returned.

I can't wash them.
I can't wear them.
But I can't let go either.

This is the worst part —
not the crying,
but the quiet inventory of everything you forgot to take with you.

—Noah

Quote
*"Grief doesn't shout.
It whispers from your closet
and brushes its teeth with your memory."*

Letter 9:
I Stopped Playing Our Song

I can't listen to that song anymore.
The one we used to dance to
in the middle of the kitchen
at 2 AM.

You said the lyrics felt like home.
Now they feel like trespassing.

I played it yesterday by mistake.
First chord —
and my chest cracked open.

I sat down on the floor.
Just like I used to.
But this time, no arms wrapped around me.
No warm laugh.
No off-beat humming.

Just a cold tile
and a colder truth:
you're never coming back.

I didn't even finish the song.

I just pressed skip.
And then cried
for everything we never made it to.

—Noah

Quote
"There are songs I'll never play again.
Not because I hate them —
but because they remember you louder than I do."

Letter 10:
The Call I Never Made

I stared at your number for 22 minutes.

I didn't call.

I don't even know why I was holding my phone like that.
Thumb hovering over your name
like it still had a chance.

I remembered how you used to answer on the third ring.
Always the third.
You said it gave you time to decide
if you were ready to hear my voice.

I waited anyway.

But this time, I didn't press "dial."
Because I was scared.

Not of what you'd say.

But of hearing the voice
that used to sound like home
now sounding like a stranger.

So I turned my phone face down,
and cried into a pillow
that still remembers your scent.

—Noah

Quote

"Sometimes we don't call.
Not because we've moved on —
but because we know they have."

Letter 11:
You Promised You'd Stay

You once held my face in your hands
and whispered,
"I won't leave. I promise."

I believed you.
God, I believed you.

You said love wasn't something that disappears.
But maybe it is.
Maybe it has a timer.
Maybe it runs out
just when you're starting to feel safe.

I don't blame you.

I blame the words we said too early.
The ones we carved into air
as if they'd last longer than our breath.

I still sleep on one side of the bed,
because the other side feels sacred.

You promised to stay.

I promised to never stop trying.

We both lied.

—Noah

Quote
"Some promises don't break like glass.
They fade like ink —
slowly, silently, until you forget what was written."

Letter 12:
I Found Your Hair Tie Today

I was cleaning the drawer we never organized.
And there it was —
your black hair tie.

Tangled in an old movie ticket.
The one from our first date.
You laughed too loud in that cinema.
I loved that.

I picked it up like it was fragile.
Held it between two fingers
like it might still hold the shape of your wrist.

Funny how something so small
can pull a scream from your chest.

I don't know why I kept it.
Maybe because letting go
feels like telling the universe
you didn't matter.

But you did.
You still do.

Even if your hair tie
is all I have left to hold.

—Noah

Quote
"Some heartbreaks live in drawers —
hidden in things that should've meant nothing,
but now mean everything

Letter 13:
The Day You Walked Out

You didn't shout.
You didn't slam the door.
You just... picked up your bag
and said,
"I think this is where it ends."

I stood still.
I didn't cry.
I just watched you tie your hair
like you always did when you were nervous.

You looked around once,
like you were searching for a reason to stay.
But maybe you didn't find one.

Or maybe I wasn't enough of one.

The room has never felt full since.
I still hear the sound of your footsteps
walking away.

Sometimes I replay them
just to feel the last moment you were mine.

—Noah

Quote

"Some people don't leave all at once.
They leave one step at a time,
and the last one is just the quietest."

Letter 14:
Our Anniversary, Alone

It would've been three years today.

I bought two cups of chai.
Just like we used to.
Strong. No sugar.

I sat on that bench you loved.
The one under the broken streetlight.
The same spot where you first kissed me
without asking.

I waited for a while.
Not because I thought you'd come.
But because that's what I always did —
wait for you.

You didn't show up.
The tea got cold.
So did the sky.

I threw your cup away.
Mine too.

Because some rituals
just hurt too much to keep doing alone.

—Noah

Quote
"Anniversaries don't die with love.
They keep showing up
even when the person doesn't."

Letter 15:
I Tried Loving Someone Else

I met someone new.

She smiled like sunlight.
She laughed without apology.
She asked questions you never asked.

And still —
all I saw was your shadow
hiding behind her voice.

She touched my hand
and I flinched.
Not because it hurt —
but because it didn't feel like you.

I kissed her.
My eyes stayed open.

She didn't deserve that.
She didn't deserve
to be measured against a memory.

I'm sorry.

I'm still bleeding,
but I keep pretending it's a scar.

—Noah

Quote

*"Sometimes, moving on feels more cruel
than holding on —
especially when your heart still answers to their
name."*

Letter 16:
I Wish You Lied

You could've said
you didn't love me anymore.
You could've made me hate you.
I would've preferred that.

But you left with kindness.
And that's what broke me.

You said,
"You deserve someone who sees you."
But I was looking at you the whole time.
Every day.
Every hour.
Even when you looked away.

You said,
"This is what's best for both of us."

No.
It was best for you.
I'm still here
trying to unlove someone
who left gently.

That's the worst kind of goodbye —
the one that doesn't give you a reason
to stop hoping.

—Noah

Quote
"Some goodbyes are soft —
but they hurt harder
because they don't give you someone to blame."

Letter 17:
I Sat With My Childhood Today

I found an old photo of myself today.
Six years old.
Sitting alone on a swing.
Smiling —
but not really.

I stared at that kid
and whispered,
"I'm sorry."

He didn't know
that every time he got close to love,
it would walk away.

He didn't know
he'd keep choosing people
who would leave like shadows at sunset.

He didn't know
he'd give his whole heart
and get half a goodbye in return.

I wanted to hold him.
Tell him he was enough.
Tell him not to beg.
Not to break himself
just to be kept.

I wanted to tell him
she wouldn't stay.
None of them do.

—Noah

Quote
"The hardest part of healing
is realizing you've been grieving since childhood."

Letter 18:
The 3AM Version of Me

It's 3:12 AM.

The walls are quiet.
The fan keeps clicking.
My phone is face down.
Like I'm punishing it
for not lighting up with your name.

I wonder if you're sleeping.
Peacefully.
While I'm here, wide awake,
trying not to cry loud enough
to wake the neighbors.

I miss the version of me
who believed you loved him.
The one who used to hum our song while brushing his teeth.
The one who left one side of the bed untouched.
Still does.

I thought time would heal this.
But time is just a clock

*reminding me how long it's been
since I last mattered to someone.*

—Noah

Quote
*"3AM is when love becomes a ghost,
and you become the only one left
trying to bring it back."*

Letter 19:
You Never Looked Back

You didn't even turn around.
Not once.

You walked out the gate,
down the stairs,
past the guard who always smiled at us.
You didn't wave.
Didn't pause.
Didn't hesitate.

Like I was a chapter
you finished reading
with no need to re-read.

I stood by the window
for 20 minutes after you left.
I counted the footsteps.
Hoped for one — just one —
to return.

But nothing.

The city moved on.
And you did too.

I was the only one
who stayed frozen in the moment
you decided
I wasn't worth staying for.

—Noah

Quote
"Some people leave so cleanly,
it makes you wonder
if they were ever really yours."

Letter 20:
I Miss Your Voice the Most

Not your face.
Not your touch.
Not even your smile.

Your voice.

The way you said my name
like it meant something.
Like I meant something.

You once left me a voice note —
just five seconds long.
You said,
"Text me when you get home, okay?"

I still have it.
I play it sometimes
just to feel like someone cares if I get home at all.

You had a way of making "okay"
sound like a promise.
Even though you broke every other one.

Your voice is fading in my memory now.
That's what hurts the most.

Losing the sound
that once held me together.

—Noah

Quote
"Some people live in your head.
Others live in your heartbeat.
But the hardest to forget
are the ones who lived in your voice."

Letter 21:
I Almost Gave Up Today

Today was heavy.

I didn't eat.
Didn't shower.
Didn't speak to anyone.

I just lay on the floor,
watching the fan spin above me,
wondering what it would feel like
to disappear.

No messages.
No missed calls.
Not even a spam email.

You once said,
"If anything ever happens to you, I'll know."
Well —
I almost didn't make it today.
And no one knew.

Not even you.

I wanted you to check in.
To feel something.
To care — even a little.
But silence stayed louder than love.

I'm still here.
But I don't know why.

—Noah

Quote

"Sometimes we don't want to die.
We just want someone to notice we're fading."

I Laughed in Public Today

I laughed today.
In front of people.

Someone told a joke,
and I laughed.

Loud.
Like I meant it.
Like I wasn't broken inside.

They smiled back,
thinking I was healing.
Thinking I was okay now.

But inside...
I was screaming your name.

Do you know what it feels like
to laugh with your mouth
and cry with your soul?

I came home and collapsed in the bathroom.
Pressed my forehead to the cold tile.
Let the sobs come like waves
that had been waiting all day to crash.

I'm tired of acting like I survived you.
I didn't.
I'm just really good at wearing your goodbye
like it doesn't still bleed.

—Noah

Quote
"Sometimes the loudest laughs
come from the people
who've forgotten how to feel safe in silence."

Letter 23:
I Deleted Our Photos

I went through my gallery today.
Found all the pictures of us.
Us smiling.
Us pretending.

You holding my hand.
Me believing it meant forever.

I stared at each one
like they were little pieces of a lie
I once called love.

My thumb hovered over "Delete"
so many times.
But I kept hesitating.
Because once they're gone,
it's like we never happened.

And maybe we didn't.
Not really.
Not in the way I thought.

But I deleted them.
Every single one.
And I cried.
Not because I missed you.
But because I couldn't believe
how happy I looked next to someone
who left so easily.

—Noah

Quote
"The worst heartbreak
isn't in losing someone.
It's in realizing
they never mourned losing you."

Letter 24:
You Didn't Grieve Me

I lost you like a person dies.
In stages.
Denial.
Anger.
Desperation.
Stillness.

But you...
You didn't lose me at all.

You didn't break.
Didn't check in.
Didn't flinch when I vanished.

You moved on
like I was never the reason
you once smiled at your phone screen.

I died a little every day after you.
You were just... fine.

And that's what kills me.
Not that you're gone.

But that I was easier to forget
than I ever imagined.

I grieved you like a funeral.
You deleted me like a file.

—Noah

Quote
"I buried you with flowers.
You buried me with silence."

Letter 25:
The Night I Almost Texted You 'I Miss You'

I almost texted you tonight.
I even typed the words:
"I miss you."

Then I stared at them
for a long time.
So long the screen went dark.

Because the truth is —
I don't miss you.
I miss who I was
when I believed you loved me.

I miss waking up
thinking someone out there
was praying for me to smile.

I miss feeling chosen.

But I didn't send it.
Because I knew you'd read it,

smile,
and go back to forgetting me.

And I...
I deserve more than being a notification
you swipe away.

So I deleted it.
And cried anyway.

—Noah

Quote
"The worst thing isn't not sending the message.
It's knowing it wouldn't have changed anything if
you did."

Letter 26:
I Can't Listen to Love Songs Anymore

Every song sounds like you.
Even the ones you never liked.

Every chorus reminds me
of how you once looked at me
like I was everything.

Now I fast-forward through every love song.
Skip the soft ones.
Mute the lyrics that say forever.

Because forever meant nothing to you.
And music still believes in it.

I used to dance in the kitchen with you.
Now I can't even boil water
without feeling like love is mocking me.

Even silence is safer.
Because silence doesn't lie.
You did.

—Noah

Quote

"Love songs are written for people who stayed.
I only know the music
that ends too soon."

Letter 27:
I Stopped Believing in Love

Tonight, I saw a couple holding hands.
They looked happy.
And I hated them for it.

Not because they smiled.
But because I used to be them.
Until I wasn't.

I used to believe love was soft.
A place to land.
A home.

Now I believe love is a trick.
A beautiful lie wrapped in warm words.
A story you write
for someone who throws it away
before they finish the last chapter.

You made me believe in forever.
And then you left
like it was nothing.

I don't believe in love anymore.
And honestly,
I miss the fool I used to be.

At least he had hope.

—Noah

Quote
"She didn't just take your love.
She took the version of you
that still believed in it."

Letter 28:
I Talked to God About You

Tonight, I looked up
and whispered your name to the stars.
Then I whispered it again —
like maybe God didn't hear me the first time.

I don't pray much anymore.
But I prayed tonight.
Not for you to come back.
Not even for peace.
Just for one answer:

Did she ever really love me,
or was I just filling space
until she found better?

The sky didn't say anything.
But the wind felt colder.
And the silence
sounded like the word "no."

I asked God if this pain would end.
And all He gave me
was another morning.

—Noah

Quote

"I stopped asking for her to come back.
Now I just ask
to forget how it felt when she loved me."

Letter 29:
The Day I Screamed Into a Pillow

I finally broke today.
No poetry.
No quiet.
Just pain.

I screamed into a pillow
until my throat burned.
Until I felt something
other than numbness.

I slammed the door.
Punched the mattress.
Fell to the floor
like I'd been holding my breath
since the day you left.

I kept saying your name
like it was a spell
that might undo all of this.

But nothing changed.
The room stayed empty.
The echo didn't answer back.

And when I stopped,
when I couldn't scream anymore —
I realized I was crying your name
like a man begging the sea
to bring back a ship
that already sank.

—Noah

Quote
"Sometimes you don't cry
because you're hurt.
You cry
because it's the only thing left you can do."

Letter 30:
I Don't Recognize Myself Anymore

I saw a photo of me
from a year ago.
Before you.

I looked happy.
Light.
Like someone who still trusted the world.

Now when I pass a mirror,
I see someone else.
Someone tired.
Someone small.

I've stopped talking to people.
Stopped smiling when it doesn't feel real.
I delete messages without opening them.
I sleep too much
or not at all.

You didn't just break my heart —
you took pieces of me
I didn't know were yours to take.

I'm trying to rebuild.
But I don't know what I'm rebuilding.
I don't even know who I am anymore.

—*Noah*

Quote
"Some people don't leave with a goodbye.
They leave by changing who you are
until you don't recognize yourself."

Letter 31:
Maybe It Was My Fault

Some nights,
I replay everything.
Not the good moments —
the bad ones.

The times I didn't say enough.
The times I said too much.
The times I shut down
when you needed me open.

Maybe you left
because I made it too hard to stay.

I keep wondering if I was too quiet,
too emotional,
too slow to heal,
too hard to love.

Maybe I made loving me
feel like a burden
you weren't strong enough to carry.

I hate myself sometimes
for not being better.
For not seeing the end coming.
For loving you in the only way I knew —
which clearly wasn't enough.

I still don't know what I did wrong.
But you left.
So it had to be something.

—Noah

Quote
"Some heartbreaks don't come with answers —
just questions that rot inside you."

Letter 32:
I Should've Held You Tighter That Night

Do you remember that night on the balcony?

It was raining.
You stood with your arms crossed,
looking like you wanted to leave
but didn't know how to say it.

I should've pulled you into my arms.
Should've kissed the doubt off your lips.
Should've told you I loved you
without waiting for the perfect moment.

But I didn't.
I stood in the doorway,
asking if you were okay,
like a stranger.

You said, "I'm fine."
But I should've known.
I should've known "fine"
meant "hold me before I disappear."

*That was the last time
you stood that close to me.*

*And I let you slip through my fingers
like rain.*

—Noah

Quote
*"We always realize too late
which moments were our last chances."*

Letter 33:
I Was Never Enough — Was I?

I gave you all I had.
Even the broken parts.
Especially the broken parts.

I let you see the dark corners.
The childhood scars.
The fears I never told anyone.

I thought
if I gave you the raw truth,
you'd love me more.

But maybe I gave too much.
Maybe I scared you.

Or maybe I was never enough.
Not smart enough.
Not stable enough.
Not lovable enough.

And now I wonder —
was I ever truly chosen?

Or was I just
the easiest person to leave?

Because that's who I keep becoming.
The one they leave
when they remember
they deserve more.

—Noah

Quote
"It's not the leaving that breaks you.
It's the feeling that
you were never worth staying for."

Letter 34:
The Last Goodbye You Don't Remember

You left me twice.
The first time — with silence.
The second — with a smile.

I remember the last time I saw you.
You waved.
Like it was just another day.
Like I was just another person.

And I smiled back.
Because I didn't know
how to fall apart gracefully.

But after you turned the corner,
I stood there for ten minutes,
blinking too hard
because I didn't want strangers to see me cry.

You walked away light.
I walked home like a funeral
with no one else attending.

That was the day
I learned goodbyes aren't always loud.
Sometimes, they're so soft
you don't even know they've happened
until your heart stops being called home.

—Noah

Quote
"Not all goodbyes sound like doors closing.
Some sound like nothing.
And that's what hurts more."

Letter 35:
I Still Remember the Way You Looked at Me Once

There was this one night
you looked at me like I was the only thing in the universe
that made sense.

I think about that a lot.
Not because I miss the moment —
but because I miss the person
you were in it.

You had tears in your eyes,
but your smile didn't shake.
You said,
"Don't you dare give up on yourself."

Funny, right?
You said that
and then gave up on us.

I replay that look in my head
like a scene from a movie
that ends too early.

Because maybe, just maybe,
for that one second,
you really did love me.

And maybe
that second
has to be enough.

—Noah

Quote
"Sometimes, a single moment
is all the proof you have
that love was real."

Letter 36:
I Heard Your Name Today

Someone said your name today.

Not in a special way.
Just casual.
Just part of a story
you weren't even in.

But my chest locked up.
My hands went cold.
And the world paused
like your ghost had walked into the room.

It's strange
how your name still feels like glass
lodged in my throat.

I wonder if my name
does that to you too.
If you ever flinch
when someone reminds you
of the boy who worshipped you
and broke himself doing it.

Probably not.

*You say a name enough times
and it just becomes noise.*

*But yours?
It's still the loudest sound
in my quietest hours.*

—Noah

Quote
*"Their name becomes a knife
long after they've stopped using it."*

Letter 37:
You Don't Miss Me — I Know That Now

You don't miss me.
I know that now.

Not because you told me.
But because you didn't.

No accidental messages.
No "I heard our song today."
No late-night texts
asking if I still think about you.

You don't wonder
if I'm eating,
sleeping,
breathing through the mess you left.

And that's what breaks me.
You forgot me
so easily.

And I...
I still flinch
when someone wears your shade of lipstick.

I still sit on your side of the bed
when I need to feel close to you.

But you don't miss me.
I know that now.
And I wish I didn't.

—Noah

Quote
"Missing someone who doesn't miss you back
is like praying to a god
that stopped listening."

Letter 38:
My Birthday Felt Like a Funeral

It was my birthday today.

No candles.
No calls.
Not from you.

I waited until midnight
thinking maybe
you'd remember.
Maybe your heart would whisper
the date
your love used to celebrate.

But the clock changed.
And nothing came.

So I sat in the dark
with one cupcake
and a lighter.

I didn't even sing to myself.

It felt wrong
to celebrate a life

that still aches for someone
who isn't aching back.

My birthday felt like a funeral.
Because the one person
I wanted to hear from
wasn't coming.

—Noah

Quote
"Some birthdays feel more like endings
than beginnings."

Letter 39:
I Feel Invisible Now

It's strange.
I used to feel seen with you.
Understood.
Even loved.

Now I feel like I don't exist.
Like I'm walking through this world
wrapped in fog.

People talk to me
but they don't really see me.
Not the way you did.
Not the way I needed.

I pass mirrors
and sometimes I don't even look.
Because I'm scared
I'll find nothing there.

That's what your absence did.
It made me
disappear.

Not all at once.
But slowly.
Quietly.
Until even I forgot
what I looked like when I was loved.

—Noah

Quote
"The cruelest part of heartbreak
is how it makes you invisible
to yourself."

Letter 40:
I'm Not Sad Anymore — I'm Just Empty

I don't cry anymore.

I thought that meant I was healing.
But I've learned
there's something worse than sadness.

It's emptiness.

I don't feel the pain as sharply now —
but that's not comfort.
It's absence.

Like my heart got tired
of being broken,
and just... shut off.

People say,
"Time will heal you."

But what if time
just turns you into someone
who no longer feels?

I'm not sad anymore.
I'm just quiet.
Detached.
Like love was a language
I forgot how to speak.

—Noah

Quote
"Sometimes the scariest part of grief
is when it stops hurting —
and starts feeling like nothing."

Letter 41:
I Pretended to Be Okay Today

I went out today.
Laughed with people.
Ate a full meal.
Told jokes.
Even made plans for next week.

They said I seemed better.

They don't know
that when I got home,
I sat on the floor for an hour
and just… stared.

At the wall.
At the air.
At nothing.

I've gotten good
at wearing a version of me
that looks okay.

I know how to nod at the right time,
smile without shaking,

say "I'm fine"
without choking on it.

But every night,
I take off the mask
and I'm back here —
in this space where your name
still echoes.

—Noah

Quote
"Some people heal in public.
But fall apart
the moment the door closes."

Letter 42:
I Let Go of Something Today

Not you.
Not yet.

But something.

I finally stopped checking
if you viewed my stories.
Stopped reading old chats.
Stopped hoping you'd call.

It wasn't dramatic.
No big decision.
Just... quiet.
Like something inside me exhaled
for the first time in months.

I didn't let go of you.
But I let go of the idea
that I still mattered to you.

And that, somehow,
felt like progress.

A wound doesn't stop being a wound
just because you stop picking at it.

But today,
I let it rest.

—Noah

Quote
"Healing doesn't always feel like hope.
Sometimes, it just feels
like giving up the illusion of being loved."

Letter 43:
I Saw You With Someone Else

I saw you today.

You were laughing.
With him.
Not in the way you used to laugh with me.
This laugh was lighter.
Free.

Like I never happened.

He touched your arm
and you didn't flinch.
You leaned into it.
Smiled like his name lived in your bones now.

And me?
I stood frozen behind a parked car
like a ghost
watching the world
forget it ever haunted anyone.

I don't hate you.
But I hate how easy it was
for you to move on.

How quickly I became
a story you no longer read.

I walked home
with your laughter stuck in my ears
like a song I never wanted to hear again.

—Noah

Quote
"Some heartbreaks don't end when they leave.
They end
when you watch them fall in love again."

Letter 44:
You Replaced Me — I Can't Even Replace My Sleep

You found someone new.
Faster than I expected.
Faster than I healed.

He probably texts you good morning now.
The way I used to.
He probably knows your coffee order,
the exact way you like your noodles,
and how you cry during Pixar movies.

He's living in all the places
I still visit in my head.

You've replaced me.
And me?
I can't even replace my sleep.

Nights are just hours
where I try not to remember
what it felt like
to be the person you whispered forever to.

I hope he gives you everything I couldn't.
And I hope
you never leave him the way you left me.

But mostly...
I hope he knows
he's holding something
that once held my whole world.

—Noah

Quote 9
"*They move on to someone new.*
You move on to someone you're not sure you'll ever be again."

Letter 45:
Dear Me — I'm Sorry

Not to her.

To me.

I'm sorry
for every time I said "I'm fine"
when I wasn't.

For letting someone else's silence
become louder than my own needs.

For waiting by the phone,
for refreshing her profile,
for writing love Letters
to someone who forgot how to read them.

I'm sorry for holding in tears
just to look strong.
For breaking quietly
so no one would have to carry the weight of me.

But I see you now.
Broken.

Bruised.
Still here.

And I swear,
if no one else chooses you,
I will.

From now on,
I write for you.

—Noah

Quote
"The most important apology
is the one you owe yourself."

Letter 46: I Cleaned the Room Today

Your scarf was still hanging
on the back of the door.
That pale blue one
you wore on cold mornings
and forgot here the day you left.

I almost threw it away.
But instead,
I folded it neatly
and packed it in a box.

The bed is finally made.
The cup is gone.
The bathroom smells like lemon again —
not you.

It took me four months
to clean this room.
Not because it was dirty,
but because it still smelled
like the version of us I wasn't ready to erase.

But today,
I opened the windows.

And maybe,
for the first time,
the air felt like it belonged to me again.

—Noah

Quote
"Healing doesn't happen when you forget them.
It happens when their memory stops owning your
space."

Letter 47:
I Laughed — And Didn't Feel Guilty

It was a stupid joke.
Something about pineapples.
But I laughed.

I laughed like it didn't hurt anymore.
Like I didn't have a hundred memories
waiting behind my eyes.

And you know what?

I didn't feel guilty.

I didn't stop mid-laugh
and wonder if you'd be proud
or if I was "moving on too soon."

I just laughed.
Loud.
Real.

And no — I'm not healed.
I still miss you
in songs, in smells, in rain.

But for one minute today,
you weren't in the room.
And I didn't miss you for it.

—Noah

Quote
"The first time you smile without guilt
is the first time your heart takes its own side."

Letter 48:
I Didn't Think About You Until Now

Today passed.
Fully.

I woke up.
Went outside.
Made tea.
Read three chapters of a book.
Called my mom.

And I didn't think about you.

Not once.
Not until now —
writing this Letter.

That used to scare me.
The idea of forgetting.
But now I see
it's not forgetting.

It's living.

You'll always be a chapter.
But I don't have to stay stuck on the page.

I loved you.
God, I did.

But now I'm trying to love something else —
my life.

—Noah

Quote
"You'll always be part of my story.
But I'm finally turning the page."

Letter 49:
I Spoke Kindly to Myself Today

I looked in the mirror
and didn't flinch.

I didn't scan my face
for what she didn't want.
I didn't compare myself
to who she chose after me.

I just looked.
At the tired eyes.
The healing skin.
The boy who survived himself.

And I said,
"You're doing okay."

That's all.
Not a grand speech.
Not a lie.

Just honesty.
Soft.
Forgiving.

And for the first time,
it felt like I was on my own side.

—Noah

Quote
"The most powerful words
are the ones we finally say
to ourselves."

Letter 50:
I Felt Peace Today — For No Reason

There was no big moment.
No sunrise epiphany.
No Letter from you
saying sorry.

Just silence.
And me —
sitting on the floor,
drinking tea,
watching light spill through the window.

And I felt… okay.

Not joyful.
Not healed.
But not broken either.

Just still.

I used to think peace
was something someone gave you.

Now I think
it's what you find

when you stop asking
for things that won't come back.

—*Noah*

Quote
"Peace isn't loud.
It's the moment you stop begging
for answers."

Letter 51:
To the One I Haven't Met Yet

If you're reading this someday —
if I'm lucky enough to hold your hand
without shaking —
I want you to know this:

I once loved someone
with everything I had.
And she left.

And for a long time,
I didn't believe love was real anymore.
I didn't believe I was lovable.

But I'm writing this
because I'm trying again.
Because I believe
you might be different.

I don't need perfect.
I don't need promises.

Just presence.
Just truth.

Just someone who stays
when the rain comes.

And if you're that person —
I'll love you softly,
honestly,
like someone who remembers
what it cost him to hope again.

—Noah

Quote
"Love isn't about forgetting the pain.
It's about finding someone
worth hoping for again."

Letter 52:
You Taught Me What I Didn't Deserve

I don't hate you.
Not anymore.

But I won't thank you either.
Not for the pain.
Not for the lesson.
Not for the nights I held my breath
because I didn't want to wake up hurting again.

They say heartbreak teaches you.
And yes — I've learned.

I've learned what *not* to accept.
What silence really means.
What begging for love
does to your soul.

I thought you were my forever.
You were just a mirror
showing me the parts of me
I still needed to protect.

So no,
I don't hate you.

But I'm finally done
building altars for people
who only visit when they're lonely.

—Noah

Quote
"Sometimes, they don't break your heart.
They just show you where it was already cracked."

Letter 53:
You're Just A Story Now

Someone asked me about you today.

I smiled.
Said, "Yeah, she was important once."

That was it.

No tremble in my voice.
No lump in my throat.
Just a calm breeze
where there used to be a storm.

You're a story now.
A soft one.
Still sad.
But no longer bleeding.

And me?
I'm the page that kept turning.

I still remember your laugh.
But it doesn't echo the way it used to.

And that,
somehow,
is enough.

—Noah

Quote
*"You never stop remembering them.
You just stop remembering in pain."*

Letter 54:
I Don't Need Closure Anymore

I used to dream of one last talk.
One final message.
A moment where you'd say,
"I'm sorry. You mattered."

But now,
I don't need it.

You're gone.
And I'm still here.
Still breathing.
Still standing.

That's enough proof
that I didn't need your closure.
I just needed my own strength.

I thought you were the final chapter.
Turns out,
you were just the middle.

And I still have pages left to write.

—Noah

Quote

"Closure isn't something they give you.
It's the door you learn to close
when they never come back."

Letter 55:
I Took Myself on a Walk Today

It wasn't for anyone.
No photos.
No captions.
No pretending.

Just me.
Walking through a quiet street.
Feeling the wind.
Looking at the trees.
Letting the sun touch my face
like it still remembered who I was.

I didn't wear the cologne you liked.
I didn't think about how you'd hold my hand.

I just walked.
Not to escape.
Not to prove anything.

But because my legs worked.
And my heart did too.
And that was reason enough to keep going.

—Noah

Quote

"The smallest joys
feel like miracles
when you've been drowning in grief."

Letter 56:
I Fell in Love with Silence Again

There was a time
when silence terrified me.
It reminded me of you.
Of unanswered calls,
read receipts,
empty chairs.

But today,
I sat in silence
and it didn't hurt.

No flashbacks.
No ghosts.

Just breath.
Just a ceiling.
Just a body
that made it through
things it thought would kill it.

I used to fill the silence with your name.
Now I fill it
with peace.

And for once,
silence isn't loneliness.
It's *freedom*.

—Noah

Quote
*"Healing is when the quiet
no longer sounds like their absence."*

Letter 57:
I Think I'm Ready to Love Again Someday

Not today.
Not tomorrow.
But someday.

Someday I'll meet someone
and I won't compare them to you.
I won't flinch
when they ask about my past.

I'll tell them,
"I loved someone once.
And it broke me.
But I survived."

I won't be scared of love this time.
Because this time,
I'll bring the version of me
who knows how to stay soft
without getting lost.

If they leave —
I'll still have myself.

And that's how I know
I'm ready again.

Because love,
from now on,
will never mean losing me too.

—Noah

Quote
*"The most beautiful kind of healing
is when you trust your heart
to open again."*

Letter 58:
Thank You for the Hurt

I hated you for a long time.
For leaving.
For not fighting.
For making love feel like a lesson
instead of a gift.

But now,
I don't carry hate anymore.

I carry *understanding*.

You were a part of my life.
A loud, beautiful, breaking part.
And I gave you everything I had.

You didn't stay.
But your leaving
made room for something
I didn't know I needed —
me.

So thank you.
Not for the love.

But for the hurt.
Because the hurt
became the map.

And I followed it
back to my own heart.

—Noah

Quote
*"Some people love you by breaking you.
And in the breaking,
you find your own strength."*

Letter 59:
I Forgive You

Not because you asked.
You never did.

But because carrying this pain
is too heavy now.
And I deserve lighter.

I forgive you
for the promises you made
before you knew how to keep them.

I forgive you
for not knowing how to stay.

I forgive myself, too —
for holding on too long,
for breaking quietly,
for believing love had to mean sacrifice.

Forgiveness isn't forgetting.
It's letting the pain grow wings
and fly off your chest.

And today,
I finally opened the window.

—Noah

Quote

"Forgiveness isn't for them.
It's for the version of you
that deserves to breathe again."

Letter 60:
The One I'll Never Send

This is it.
The last Letter.

Not because I've run out of things to say,
but because I've said enough.

If you ever read this —

+know that I loved you.
Truly.
Deeply.
In ways you'll never fully understand.

And I don't regret a second of it.

But I can't write to you anymore.
I'm no longer trying to hold your ghost in my hands.

You were a season.
A storm.
A song I used to hum in the dark.

But now it's morning.
And the light is finding me again.

I'm closing this chapter
not to forget you —
but to remember who I am without you.

Goodbye.
Softly,
finally,
completely.

—Noah

Quote
*"The most powerful goodbyes
are the ones whispered
when no one else is listening."*

The End.

But truly — *a beginning*.

Conclusion

To the one who survived love,
If you made it here —
thank you.
For holding my hand through the storm.
For seeing yourself in these Letters.
For feeling what I felt
and still choosing to stay.

I wrote this book to heal.
But maybe,
you needed it to remember
that even broken gods
can be beautiful
in their becoming.

Love doesn't always end in forever.
But pain, when given a voice,
can turn into poetry.
And survival, when witnessed,
becomes something sacred.

You were never too much.
You were never too weak.

You were just someone who loved
with everything they had.

And now —
you're someone who lived
to tell the story.

Keep your heart soft.
Keep going.
Keep writing your way home.

With love,
—Noah

www.ingramcontent.com/pod-product-compliance
Lightning Source LLC
LaVergne TN
LVHW041610070526
838199LV00052B/3076